THE CHARTS

Some of the designs in this book are very detailed and, due to inevitable space limitations, the charts may be shown on a comparatively small scale; in such cases, readers may find it helpful to have the particular chart with which they are currently working enlarged.

THREADS

The projects in this book were all stitched with DMC stranded cotton embroidery threads. The keys given with each chart also list thread combinations for those who wish to use Anchor or Madeira threads. It should be pointed out that the shades produced by different companies vary slightly, and it is not always possible to find identical colours in a different range.

First published in 1996 by Merehurst Limited
Ferry House, 51-57 Lacy Road, Putney, London SW15 1PR
Copyright © 1996 Merehurst Limited
ISBN 1 85391 463-0

A catalogue record for this book is available from the British Library.

Edited by Heather Dewhurst
Designed by Maggie Aldred
Photography by Marie-Louise Avery
Illustrations by John Hutchinson
Typesetting by Dacorum Type & Print, Hemel Hempstead
Colour separation by Fotographics Limited, UK – Hong Kong
Printed in Hong Kong by Wing King Tong

Merehurst is the leading publisher of craft books and has an excellent range of titles to suit all levels. Please send to the address above for our free catalogue, stating the title of this book.

CONTENTS

INTRODUCTION

Cross stitch is one of the oldest and simplest of all embroidery stitches. With the help of the instructions on this and the following pages, novices as well as the more experienced stitcher will be able to create the perfect souvenir of that most joyous of occasions – the wedding.

The wedding day itself is represented by several projects, from the wedding sampler with its pairs of silver doves and bride's token to match, to the ring cushion with its gold embroidered rings and lace trim. The card and gift tag make the giving of a wedding present extra special and the place card and almond bag would enhance any table setting.

The silver wedding is commemorated by a bell pull embroidered with lilies and a serviette and traycloth set. The ruby anniversary is celebrated with rich vibrant red roses decorating a wedding bowl and handbag mirror.

That milestone in married life, the golden wedding, can be remembered with a beautiful photograph album embroidered with mellow daisies surrounded by a lace border. Finally, sixty years of wedded bliss – the diamond wedding anniversary – is celebrated with a framed sampler, embroidered with pink and cream roses.

BASIC SKILLS

BEFORE YOU BEGIN

PREPARING THE FABRIC
Even with an average amount of handling, many evenweave fabrics tend to fray at the edges, so it is a good idea to overcast the raw edges, using ordinary sewing thread, before you begin.

THE INSTRUCTIONS
Each project begins with a full list of the materials that you will require. All the designs are worked on evenweave fabrics such as Aida, produced by Zweigart. The measurements given for the embroidery fabric include a minimum of 5cm (2in) all around to allow for stretching it in a frame and preparing the edges to prevent them from fraying.

Colour keys for stranded embroidery cottons – DMC, Anchor or Madeira – are given with each chart. It is assumed that you will need to buy one skein of each colour mentioned in a particular key, even though you may use less, but where two or more skeins are needed, this information is included in the main list of requirements.

To work from the charts, particularly those where several symbols are used in close proximity, some readers may find it helpful to have the chart enlarged so that the squares and symbols can be seen more easily. Many photocopying services will do this for a minimum charge.

Before you begin to embroider, always mark the centre of the design with two lines of basting stitches, one vertical and one horizontal, running from edge to edge of the fabric, as indicated by the arrows on the charts.

As you stitch, use the centre lines given on the chart and the basting threads on your fabric as reference points for counting the squares and threads to position your design accurately.

WORKING IN A HOOP
A hoop is the most popular frame for use with small areas of embroidery. It consists of two rings, one fitted inside the other; the outer ring usually has an adjustable screw attachment so that it can be tightened to hold the stretched fabric in place.

Hoops are available in several sizes, ranging from 10cm (4in) in diameter to quilting hoops with a diameter of 38cm (15in). Hoops with table stands or floor stands attached are also available.

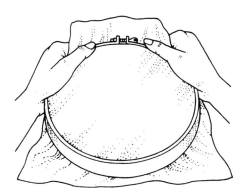

1 To stretch your fabric in a hoop, place the area to be embroidered over the inner ring and press the outer ring over it, with the tension screw released. Tissue paper can be placed between the outer ring and the embroidery, so that the hoop does not mark the fabric. Lay the tissue paper over the fabric when you set it in the hoop, then tear away the central embroidery area.

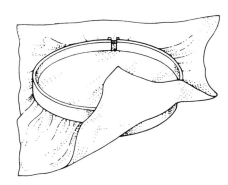

2 Smooth the fabric and, if necessary, straighten the grain before tightening the screw. The fabric should be evenly stretched.

WORKING IN A RECTANGULAR FRAME
Rectangular frames are more suitable for larger pieces of embroidery. They consist of two rollers, with tapes attached, and two flat side pieces, which slot into the rollers and are held in place by pegs or screw attachments. Available in different sizes,

either alone or with adjustable table or floor stands, frames are measured by the length of the roller tape, and range in size from 30cm (12in) to 68cm (27in).

As alternatives to a slate frame, canvas stretchers and the backs of old picture frames can be used. Provided there is sufficient extra fabric around the finished size of the embroidery, the edges can be turned under and simply attached with drawing pins (thumb tacks) or staples.

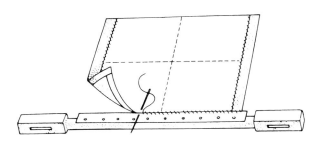

1 To stretch your fabric in a rectangular frame, cut out the fabric, allowing at least an extra 5cm (2in) all around the finished size of the embroidery. Baste a single 12mm (½in) turning on the top and bottom edges and oversew strong tape, 2.5cm (1in) wide, to the other two sides. Mark the centre line both ways with basting stitches. Working from the centre outward and using strong thread, oversew the top and bottom edges to the roller tapes. Fit the side pieces into the slots, and roll any extra fabric on one roller until the fabric is taut.

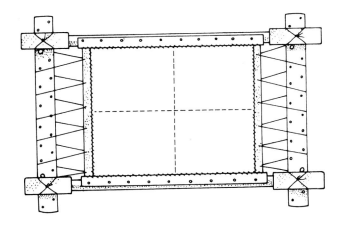

2 Insert the pegs or adjust the screw attachments to secure the frame. Thread a large-eyed needle (chenille needle) with strong thread or fine string and lace both edges, securing the ends around the intersections of the frame. Lace the webbing at 2.5cm (1in) intervals, stretching the fabric evenly.

EXTENDING EMBROIDERY FABRIC

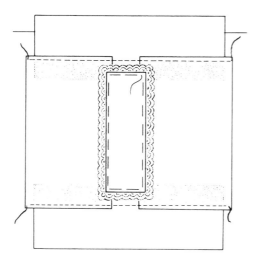

It is easy to extend a piece of embroidery fabric, such as a bookmark, to stretch it in a hoop.

● Fabric oddments of a similar weight can be used. Simply cut four pieces to size (in other words, to the measurement that will fit both the embroidery fabric and your hoop) and baste them to each side of the embroidery fabric before stretching it in the hoop in the usual way.

THE STITCHES

BACKSTITCH
Backstitch is used in the projects to give emphasis to a particular foldline, an outline or a shadow. The stitches are worked over the same number of threads as the cross stitch, forming continuous straight or diagonal lines.

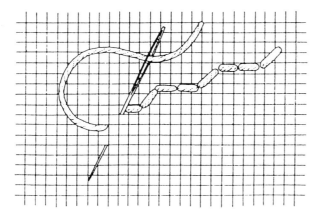

● Make the first stitch from left to right; pass the needle behind the fabric and bring it out one stitch length ahead to the left. Repeat and continue in this way along the line.

CROSS STITCH
For all cross stitch embroidery, the following two methods of working are used. In each case, neat rows of vertical stitches are produced on the back of the fabric.

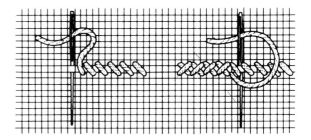

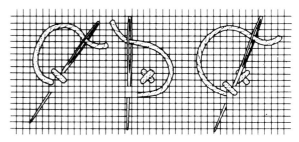

● When stitching large areas, work in horizontal rows. Working from right to left, complete the first row of evenly spaced diagonal stitches over the number of threads specified in the project instructions. Then, working from left to right, repeat the process. Continue in this way, making sure each stitch crosses in the same direction.

● When stitching diagonal lines, work downwards, completing each stitch before moving to the next. When starting a project always begin to embroider at the centre of the design and work outwards to ensure that the design will be placed centrally on the fabric.

FINISHING

MOUNTING EMBROIDERY
The cardboard should be cut to the size of the finished embroidery, with an extra 6mm (¹⁄₄in) added all round to allow for the recess in the frame.

LIGHTWEIGHT FABRICS

1 Place embroidery face down, with the cardboard centred on top, and basting and pencil lines matching. Begin by folding over the fabric at each corner and securing it with masking tape.

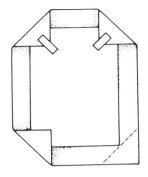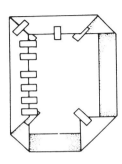

2 Working first on one side and then the other, fold over the fabric on all sides and secure it firmly with pieces of masking tape, placed about 2.5cm (1in) apart. Also neaten the mitred corners with masking tape, pulling the fabric tightly to give a firm, smooth finish.

HEAVIER FABRICS

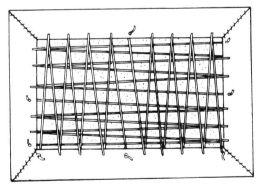

● Lay the embroidery face down, with the cardboard centred on top; fold over the edges of the fabric on opposite sides, making mitred folds at the corners, and lace across, using strong thread. Repeat on the other two sides. Finally, pull up the fabric firmly over the cardboard. Overstitch the mitred corners.

PIPED SEAMS

Contrasting piping adds a special decorative finish to a seam and looks particularly attractive on items such as cushions and cosies.

You can cover piping cord with either bias-cut fabric of your choice or a bias binding: alternatively, ready covered piping cord is available in several widths and many colours.

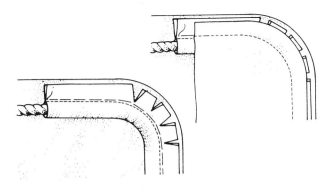

1 To apply piping, pin and baste it to the right side of the fabric, with seam lines matching. Clip into the seam allowance where necessary.

2 With right sides together, place the second piece of fabric on top, enclosing the piping. Baste and then either hand stitch in place or machine stitch, using a zipper foot. Stitch as close to the piping as possible, covering the first line of stitching.

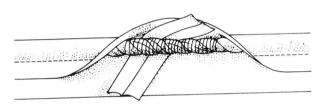

3 To join ends of piping cord together, first overlap the two ends by about 2.5cm (1in). Unpick the two cut ends of bias to reveal the cord. Join the bias strip as shown. Trim and press the seam open. Unravel and slice the two ends of the cord. Fold the bias strip over it, and finish basting around the edge.

TO MITRE A CORNER

Press a single hem to the wrong side, the same as the measurement given in the instructions. Open the hem out again and fold the corner of the fabric inwards as shown on the diagram. Refold the hem to the wrong side along the pressed line, and slip stitch in place.

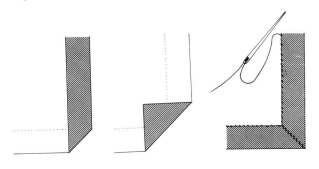

7

Wedding Sampler and Bride's Token

This charming sampler with its pairs of silver doves and the bride's keepsake worked on perforated paper, provide lasting mementoes of one of the most important days in your life.

WEDDING SAMPLER AND BRIDE'S TOKEN

YOU WILL NEED

For the Wedding Sampler, with a design area measuring 20cm (7³/₄ in) square or 88 stitches by 88 stitches, here in a frame measuring 27cm (10³/₄ in) square:

30cm (11³/₄ in) square of white, 11-count Aida fabric
Stranded embroidery cotton in the colours given in the appropriate panel
Silver thread (DMC code 278, shade 4041)
No24 tapestry needle
Strong thread, for lacing across the back
Cardboard, for mounting
Frame of your choice

For the Bride's Token, with a design area measuring 9.5cm × 7.5cm (3³/₄ in × 3 in):

13cm × 11cm (5 in × 4¹/₄ in) of white, 14-count perforated paper
Stranded embroidery cotton in the colours given in the appropriate panel
Silver thread (DMC code 278, shade 4041)
No24 tapestry needle
14cm (5 ¹/₂ in) of pink ribbon, 6mm (¹/₄ in) wide
Fabric glue
13cm × 11cm (5 in × 4¹/₄ in) of white felt

•

WEDDING SAMPLER

Prepare the fabric and stretch it in a frame as explained on page 5. Following the chart, start the embroidery at the centre of the design using three strands of cotton in the needle or a 100cm (40in) length of silver thread folded double for the cross stitch. Work each stitch over one block of fabric in each direction. Make sure that all the top crosses run in the same direction and that each row is worked into the same holes as the row before so that you do not leave a space between the rows. Embroider the names and date in backstitch, referring to the alphabet chart and using two strands of cotton in the needle.

Gently press the finished embroidery on the wrong side and mount it as explained on page 7. Choose a mount and frame to compliment your embroidery colours.

BRIDE'S TOKEN

Mark the centre of the perforated paper with a line of horizontal and vertical basting stitches. Following the chart, start the embroidery at the centre of the design using two strands of cotton in the needle or a 100cm (40in) length of silver thread folded double for the cross stitch. Handle the perforated paper carefully when sewing and ensure that you do not leave a long length of cotton at the back as this will show through. Work each stitch over one block of the paper in each direction. Work the backstitch using two strands of cotton in the needle.

Very carefully, cut around the tree about one square away from the embroidery. Do not cut too close as you will cut your stitches. Fold the ribbon in half and glue it to the wrong side of the tree at the top. Glue the tree to the piece of white felt and trim the excess felt away around the edge.

BRIDE'S TOKEN ▼		DMC	ANCHOR	MADEIRA
X	Light green	368	0214	1310
=	Dark green	320	0215	1311
O	Light pink	963	048	0608
+	Dark pink	3326	026	0504
	Grey*	414	0399	1801
S	Silver	Available from DMC only Code 278, shade 4041		

Note: bks the boughs of the tree in dark green and the initials in grey (*used for backstitch only).*

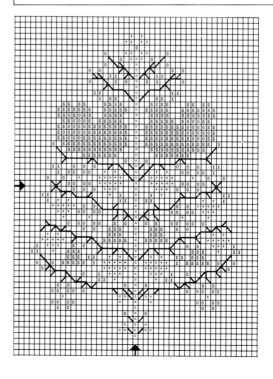

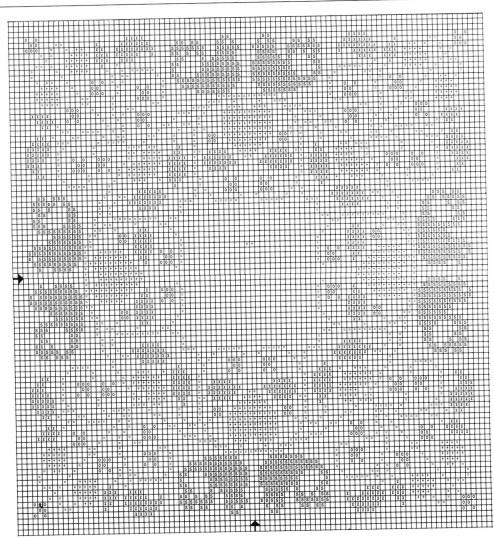

WEDDING SAMPLER ▲		DMC	ANCHOR	MADEIRA
X	Light green	368	0214	1310
=	Dark green	320	0215	1311
O	Light pink	963	048	0608
+	Dark pink	3326	026	0504
	Grey*	414	0399	1801
S	Silver	Available from DMC only Code 278, shade 4041		

Note: bks names and date in grey (*used for backstitch only).*

Wedding Accessories

Your guests will be delighted with this wedding place card and almond bag as souvenirs, while the gift tag and wedding card will show that you have put a little extra thought into your wedding present.

WEDDING ACCESSORIES

For all the projects:

*Stranded embroidery cotton in the colours
given in the appropriate panel
No24 tapestry needle
Silver thread (DMC code 278, shade 4041)
Fabric glue*

For the Wedding Place Card, with a design area
measuring 10cm × 3.5cm (4 in × 1¹/₂ in):

*6cm × 13cm (2¹/₂ in × 5in) of white, 18-count
Aida fabric
Card mount, with an aperture measuring
3.5cm × 10cm (1¹/₂ in × 4 in)*

For the Wedding Greetings Card, measuring
15cm × 20cm (6in × 8in) with a cut-out measuring
10cm × 14cm (4in × 5¹/₂ in):

*12cm × 16cm (4³/₄ in × 6¹/₄ in) of white, 26-count
evenweave linen
Purchased greetings card mount, (for
suppliers, see page 40)*

For the Gift Tag, measuring 7.5cm (3in) square with
a cut-out of 5.5cm (2¹/₄ in) in diameter:

*7cm (2³/₄ in) square of white, 26-count evenweave.
linen
Purchased gift tag (for suppliers, see page 40)*

For the Almond Bag, with a finished size of
9cm × 11.5cm (3¹/₂ in × 4¹/₂ in):

*14cm × 16cm (5¹/₂ in × 6¹/₂ in) of white, 26-count
evenweave linen
Matching sewing thread
11.5cm × 14cm (4¹/₂ in × 5¹/₂ in) of white fabric,
for backing
36cm (14in) of white broderie anglaise,
2.5cm (1in) wide
50cm (20in) of pink ribbon, 6mm (¹/₄ in) wide*

•

THE EMBROIDERY

As none of the projects is very large, they may all be
held in the hand when working the embroidery.

Following the correct chart, start the embroidery at
the centre of the design, using two strands of cotton
for all designs except the place card which is worked
with one strand of cotton for the cross stitch. Work
each stitch over either one block or two threads of
fabric in each direction. Make sure that all the top
crosses run in the same direction and that each row
is worked into the same holes as the row before so
that you do not leave a space.

For the silver crosses on the gift tag and almond
bag, use a 100cm (40in) length of silver thread
folded double, but for the silver crosses on the place
card use a 50cm (20in) length of silver thread used
singly. Work the backstitch lines on the almond
bag and place card with one strand of cotton. Blend
one 50cm (20in) length of silver thread with one
50cm (20in) length of light mauve thread for the
stitching on the almond bag and wedding card.

MAKING UP

Gently press the finished embroidery for the cards
and tags on the wrong side and trim to about 12mm
(¹/₂ in) larger than the cut-out window. Open out the
card and centre your embroidery behind the
aperture, securing with a spot of glue. Fold the card
and secure with another spot of glue.

ALMOND BAG ▼	DMC	ANCHOR	MADEIRA
⁄ Light mauve	209	0110	0803
blended with silver	(+ DMC code 278, shade 4041)		
r Medium mauve	553	098	0712
o Light green	470	0266	1502
x Medium green	937	0268	1504
c Yellow	3078	0292	0102
s Silver	Available from DMC only		
	Code 278, shade 4041		

Note: bks lines in medium green.

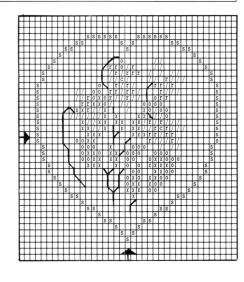

For the almond bag, trim the embroidery to measure 11.5cm × 14cm (4$\frac{1}{2}$ in × 5$\frac{1}{2}$ in). With right sides together, baste and machine stitch the embroidery to the backing fabric, stitching down the sides and across the bottom, taking a 12mm ($\frac{1}{2}$ in) seam allowance.

Turn to the right side. Turn a single 12mm ($\frac{1}{2}$ in) hem around the top. Join the short edges of the broderie anglaise with a tiny french seam, then run a gathering thread close to the straight edge of the lace. Pull up the gathers to fit and, with the right side of the lace facing the wrong side of the bag, baste and then machine stitch the broderie anglaise in place around the top. Gently steam press. Fill the bag with almonds and tie it with the ribbon.

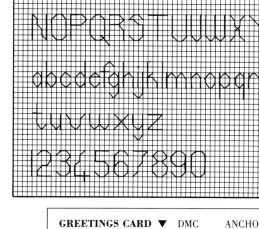

GIFT TAG ▼		DMC	ANCHOR	MADEIRA
X	Medium green	937	0268	1504
C	Yellow	3078	0292	0102
<	Light pink	3689	073	0607
+	Dark pink	3688	066	0605
r	Medium mauve	553	098	0712
S	Silver	Available from DMC only Code 278, shade 4041		

GREETINGS CARD ▼		DMC	ANCHOR	MADEIRA
O	Light green	470	0266	1502
X	Medium green	937	0268	1504
=	Dark green	3345	0269	406
/	Light mauve	209	0110	0803
	blended with silver	(+ DMC code 278, shade 4041)		
r	Medium mauve	553	098	0712
+	Dark mauve	327	0101	0805
C	Yellow	3078	0292	0102

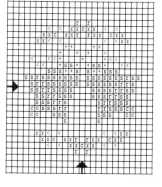

WEDDING PLACE CARD ▼		DMC	ANCHOR	MADEIRA
/	Light mauve	209	0110	0803
r	Medium mauve	553	098	0715
+	Dark mauve	327	0101	0805
C	Yellow	3078	0292	0102
>	White	Blanc	White	White
−	Light grey	762	0397	1804
V	Dark grey	415	0398	1803
S	Silver	Available from DMC only Code 278, shade 4041		
O	Light green	470	0266	1502
X	Medium green	937	0268	1504
=	Dark green	3345	0269	1406

Note: bks the name in medium green.

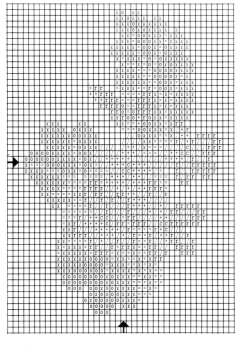

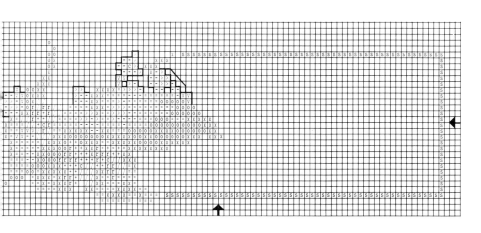

Wedding Ring Cushion

The wedding ring is a tangible
sign of everlasting love and this
beautiful wedding ring cushion
makes an ideal presentation
for the ring.

WEDDING RING CUSHION

For the Cushion, measuring 15cm (6in) square:

*25cm (10in) square of cream, 28-count
evenweave fabric
Stranded embroidery cotton in the colours given
in the panel
DMC metallic thread (code 278, shade 4024)
No24 tapestry needle
18cm (7in) square of cream fabric,
for backing
62cm (24in) of gathered lace edging,
2.5cm (1in) wide
Polyester stuffing*

•

THE EMBROIDERY

Prepare the fabric and stretch it in a frame as explained on page 5. Following the chart, start the embroidery at the centre of the design, using two strands of cotton in the needle, or a 100cm (40in) length of gold thread folded double for the cross stitch. Work each stitch over two threads of fabric in each direction, making sure that all the top crosses run in the same direction and that each row is worked into the same holes as the top or bottom of the row before so that you do not leave a space between the rows.

Embroider the single line ring in backstitch using two strands of gold thread, and backstitch the flower outlines with one strand of cotton.

MAKING UP

Gently steam press the finished embroidery on the wrong side and trim to 18cm (7in) square. Join the ends of the lace edging with a narrow french seam and pin and baste it around the edge of the right side of the embroidery. The decorative edge of the lace should face inwards and the straight edge of the lace should be parallel with the edge of the fabric, and just inside the 12mm (½in) seam allowance.

Place the backing fabric over the embroidery, with right sides facing, and baste and stitch through all three layers, stitching through the straight edge of the lace, just within the 12mm (½in) seam allowance, leaving a 7.5cm (3in) gap at one side. Turn the cushion right side out, stuff with the polyester stuffing and slip stitch to close.

WEDDING RING CUSHION ▶		DMC	ANCHOR	MADEIRA
O	Light green	3013	0842	1605
X	Medium green	3052	0861	1509
=	Dark green	3051	0862	1508
C	Cream	712	0926	2101
/	Light beige	3770	933	306
r	Dark beige	3774	881	1909
V	Yellow	745	0300	0111
S	Gold	DMC metallic thread Code 278, shade 4024		

Note: bks the single line ring with two strands of gold, and outline the flowers with dark green.

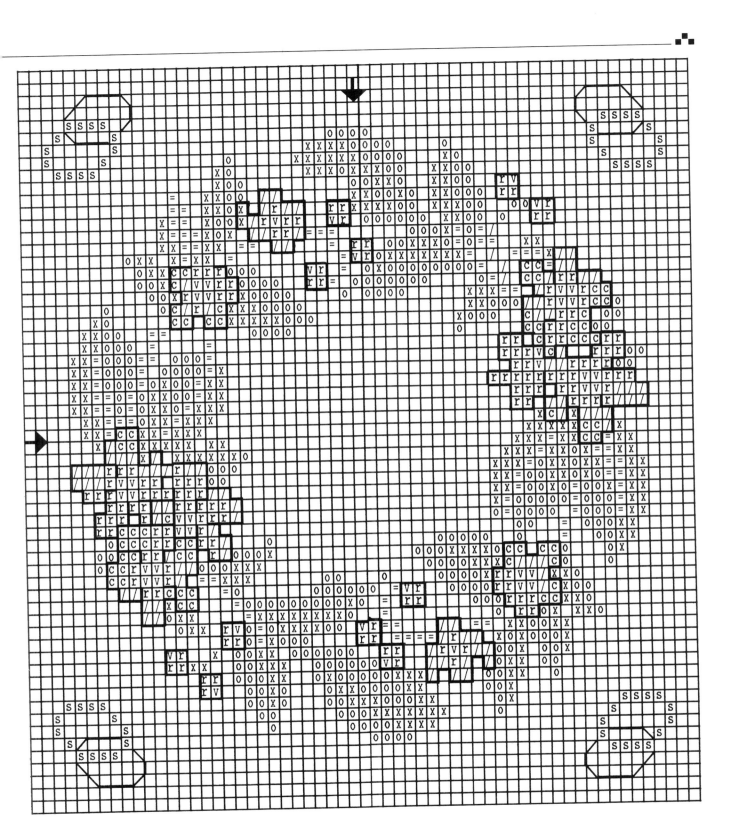

Silver Wedding Bell Pull and Card

This bell pull, with its madonna lily design and silver stitching, and the matching card celebrate 25 years of marriage.

SILVER WEDDING BELL PULL AND CARD

YOU WILL NEED

For the Silver Wedding Card, with a design area
measuring 6cm × 10.5cm (2¼in × 4¼in) or
32 stitches by 58 stitches:

16cm × 20cm (6¼in × 8in) of white,
14-count Aida fabric
Stranded embroidery cotton in the colours given
in the appropriate panel
No24 tapestry needle
Portrait card mount with an aperture measuring
7cm × 11cm (2¾in × 4½in)
Double-sided tape
Fabric glue

For the Bell Pull, with a design area measuring
36cm × 13cm (14¼in × 5¼in):

45cm (18in) strip of white Aida band, 44 stitches,
8.5cm (3½in) wide
Masking tape
Stranded embroidery cotton in the colours given
in the appropriate panel
Silver thread (DMC code 278, shade 4041)
No24 tapestry needle
A pair of bell pull fittings, 10cm (4in) wide (for
suppliers, see page 40)
Matching sewing thread

WEDDING CARD

Prepare the fabric and stretch it in a frame as
explained on page 5. Following the chart, start the
embroidery at the centre of the design using two
strands of cotton in the needle for the cross stitch.
Work each stitch over one block of fabric in each
direction. Make sure that all the top crosses run in
the same direction and that each row is worked into
the same holes as the row before so that you do not
leave a space between the rows. Work the backstitch
using one strand of cotton.

Gently press the finished embroidery on the
wrong side. Trim to about 12mm (½in) larger than
the cut-out aperture. Centre the embroidery behind
the aperture and secure with double-sided tape. Fold
the backing card inwards and stick with glue for a
secure and neat finish.

BELL PULL

Secure each end of the Aida band with masking tape
and find the centre by working a vertical and
horizontal line of basting stitches. Following the
chart, start the embroidery at the centre of the band
using two strands of cotton or a 100cm (40in) length
of silver thread folded double in the needle for the
cross stitch. Work each stitch over one block of
fabric in each direction. Make sure that all the top
crosses run in the same direction and that each row
is worked into the same holes as the row before so
that you do not leave a space. Work the backstitch
using one strand of cotton.

Gently press the work on the wrong side. Slip the
bell pull fittings over each end so that you have

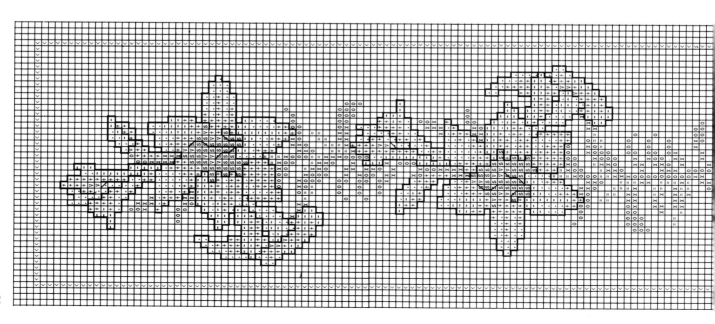

about 12mm (¹/₂in) between the line of silver stitching and the top and bottom of the bell pull. Turn the raw edge under at the top and bottom and slip stitch in place to the wrong side.

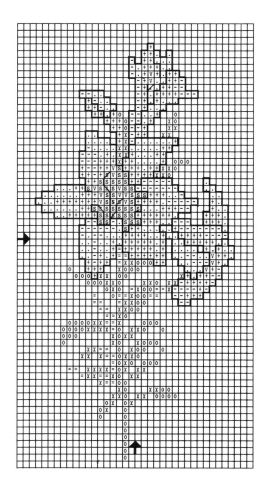

SILVER WEDDING CARD ◄		DMC	ANCHOR	MADEIRA
O	Light green	472	0253	1414
X	Medium green	471	0265	1501
=	Dark green	470	0266	1502
S	Light grey	762	0397	1804
+	Dark grey	415	0398	1803
·	White	Blanc	White	White
−	Cream	746	0926	0101
V	Apricot	948	0933	0306

Note: bks the flower outline in dark green.

BELL PULL ▼		DMC	ANCHOR	MADEIRA
O	Light green	472	0253	1414
X	Medium green	471	0265	1501
=	Dark green	470	0266	1502
S	Light grey	762	0397	1804
+	Dark grey	415	0398	1803
·	White	Blanc	White	White
−	Cream	746	0926	0101
V	Apricot	948	0933	0306
<	Silver	Available from DMC only Code 278, shade 4041		

Note: bks the flower outline in dark green.

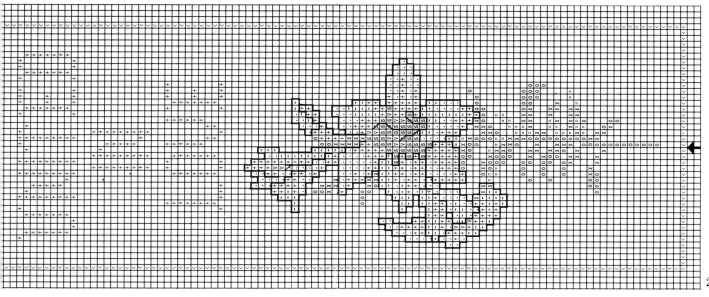

Silver Wedding Traycloth and Serviette

Afternoon tea will never be the same again with this traycloth and matching serviette embroidered with roses and ribbons.

SILVER WEDDING TRAYCLOTH AND SERVIETTE

YOU WILL NEED

For the Traycloth, measuring 33cm × 47cm
(13in × 19in):

*Purchased 26-count traycloth (for suppliers,
see page 40)*
*Stranded embroidery cotton in the colours given
in the appropriate panel*
No24 tapestry needle

For the Serviette, measuring 40cm (16in) square:

*Purchased 26-count serviette (for suppliers,
see page 40)*
*Stranded embroidery cotton in the colours given
in the appropriate panel*
No24 tapestry needle

•

PREPARING THE FABRIC

If you prefer not to use ready-prepared table linen,
buy fabric with the same thread count. To prepare
the fabric, mark a line with basting stitches 2.5cm
(1in) from the start of the fringe on the right and left
hand sides and top and bottom of the traycloth. The
point at which the lines intersect in the corners is
where you place your embroidery. For the serviette
measure 2.5cm (1in) in from the right hand and
bottom edges in one corner and mark with basting
stitches. Once again, the point at which the lines
intersect is where you place your embroidery.
Stretch the traycloth or napkin in a frame (see
page 5).

THE EMBROIDERY

Start the embroidery by positioning it following the
mark on the diagram. Using two strands of cotton in
the needle, work each cross stitch over two threads
of fabric in each direction. Make sure that all the top
crosses run in the same direction and that each row
is worked into the same holes as the row before so
that you do not leave a space between the rows.
Work the backstitch with one strand of cotton.
Gently steam press the finished embroidery on the
wrong side to remove all creases.

If you have used evenweave fabric, rather than
ready-prepared table linen, trim to the correct size
(including fringe), and withdraw a thread 12mm
(½in) in from each edge. Neatly overcast every
alternate thread, and then remove all cross threads
below the stitched line to complete the fringe.

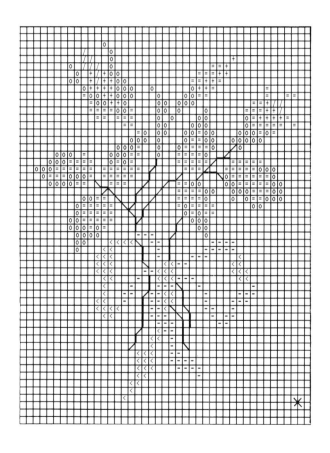

SERVIETTE ▲		DMC	ANCHOR	MADEIRA
⧄	Light peach	353	08	0304
+	Dark peach	352	09	0303
○	Light green	989	0256	1401
=	Dark green	987	0258	1403
−	Light blue	3747	117	901
<	Dark blue	794	0120	0907

Note: bks the flower stems in dark green.

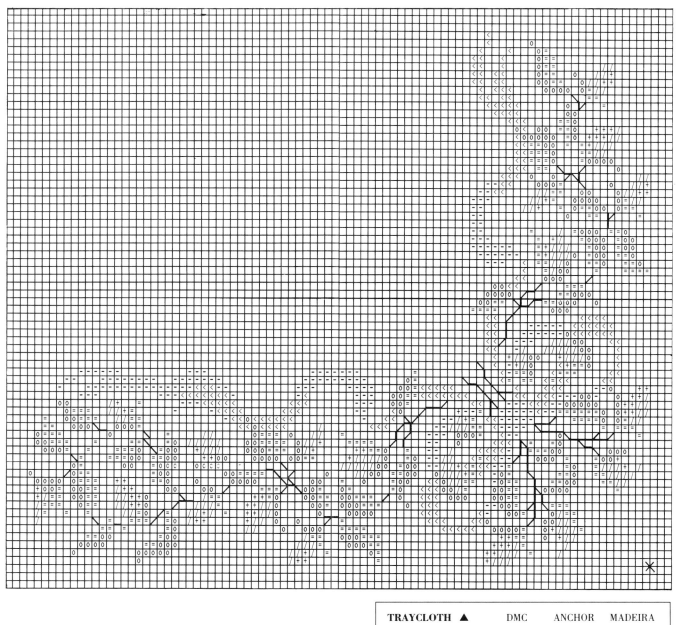

TRAYCLOTH ▲		DMC	ANCHOR	MADEIRA
╱	Light peach	353	08	0304
+	Dark peach	352	09	0303
○	Light green	989	0256	1401
=	Dark green	987	0258	1403
−	Light blue	3747	117	901
<	Dark blue	794	0120	0907

Note: bks the flower stems in dark green.

Ruby Wedding Bowl & Mirror

The vibrant colours of these ruby red roses, as fresh as the day they were cut, decorate a dressing table bowl and handbag mirror.

RUBY WEDDING BOWL AND MIRROR

YOU WILL NEED

For the Bowl, with an inset measuring
9cm (3½in) in diameter:

*12cm (4¾in) square of white, 22-count
Hardanger fabric
Stranded embroidery cotton in the colours given
in the appropriate panel
No24 tapestry needle
Glass bowl with prepared lid (for suppliers,
see page 40)*

For the Handbag Mirror, with an inset measuring
6.5cm (2½in):

*10cm (4in) square of white, 18-count
Aida fabric
Stranded embroidery cotton in the colours given
in the appropriate panel
No24 tapestry needle
Handbag mirror with prepared cover (for suppliers,
see page 40)*

•

THE EMBROIDERY

Prepare the fabric and stretch it in a frame as explained on page 5. Following the appropriate chart, start the embroidery at the centre of the design using one strand of cotton in the needle. Work each stitch over one block of fabric in each direction. Make sure that all the top crosses run in the same direction and that each row is worked into the same holes as the row before so that you do not leave a space between the rows.

MAKING UP

Gently press the finished embroidery on the wrong side. Trim the bowl lid to the size of the paper pattern that is provided with the lid and mount it as explained in the manufacturer's instructions. Trim the mirror cover to the size of the paper pattern provided and, again, mount as explained in the manufacturer's instructions.

HANDBAG MIRROR ▼		DMC	ANCHOR	MADEIRA
r	Light red	666	046	0210
v	Medium red	304	047	0509
s	Dark red	814	072	0514
x	Medium green	3347	0266	1408
=	Dark green	3345	0268	1406

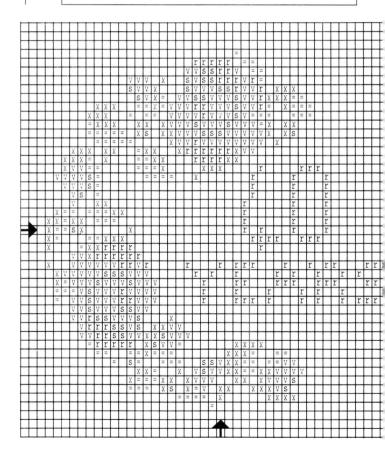

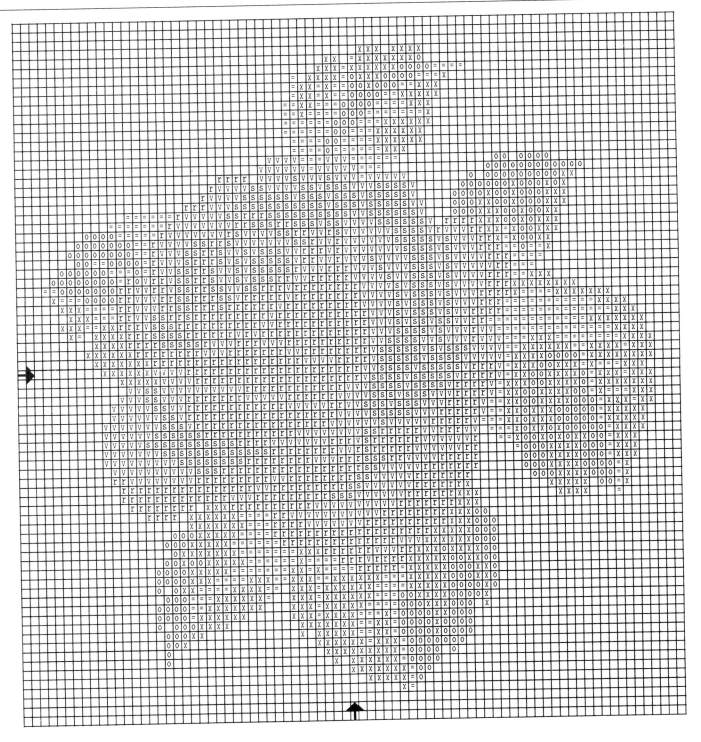

ROSE BOWL ▲	DMC	ANCHOR	MADEIRA
r Light red	666	046	0210
v Medium red	304	047	0509
s Dark red	814	072	0514
o Light green	3348	0265	1409
x Medium green	3347	0266	1408
= Dark green	3345	0268	1406

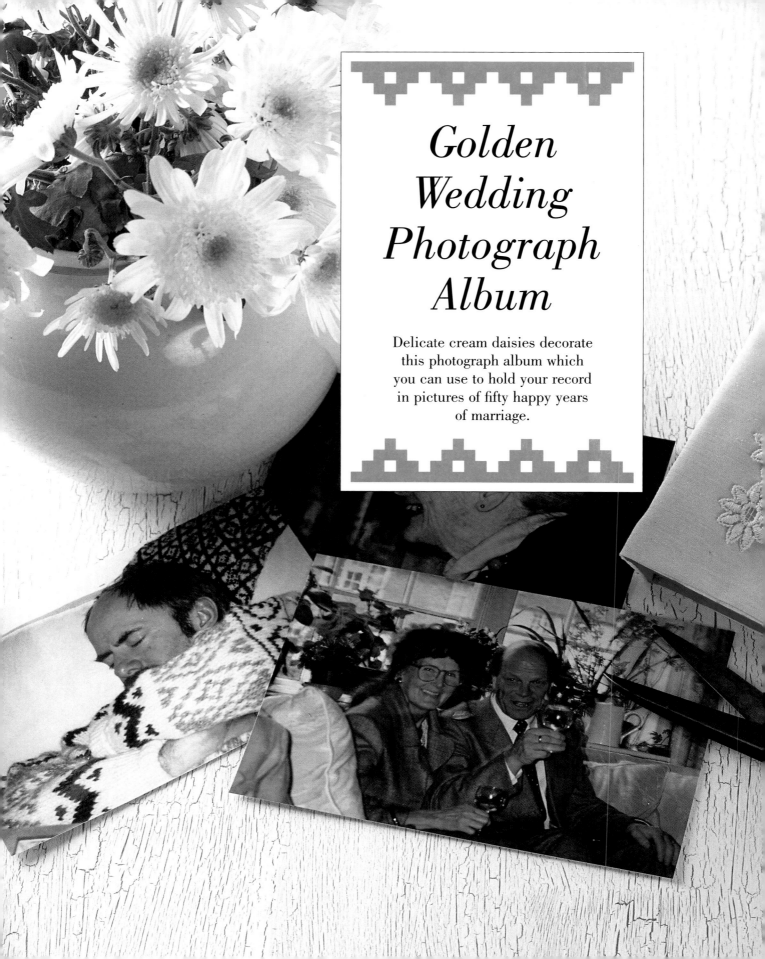

Golden Wedding Photograph Album

Delicate cream daisies decorate this photograph album which you can use to hold your record in pictures of fifty happy years of marriage.

GOLDEN WEDDING PHOTOGRAPH ALBUM

YOU WILL NEED

*33cm × 28cm (13in × 11in) of cream, 14-count
Aida fabric
Stranded embroidery cotton in the colours given
in the panel
No24 tapestry needle
Photograph album of your choice
Cream satin-type fabric, to cover photograph album
Cream backing fabric, the same size as the
cream satin
1m (40in) of cream lace daisies
Fabric glue*

•

THE EMBROIDERY

Prepare the Aida fabric and stretch it in a frame as explained on page 5. Following the chart, start the embroidery at the centre of the design, using two strands of cotton in the needle for the cross stitch. Work each stitch over a block of fabric in each direction, making sure that all the top crosses run in the same direction and that each row is worked into the same holes as the top or bottom of the row before, so that you do not leave a space between the rows. Work the backstitch using one strand of cotton in the needle.

MAKING UP

Calculate the amount of satin fabric you require by measuring your album from front cover edge to back cover edge when it is closed, adding an extra 15cm (6in), then measuring from the top edge to the bottom edge, adding an extra 2.5cm (1in). Cut out a piece of cream satin-type fabric, and cream backing fabric, following these measurements. With right sides together, baste and sew the backing fabric and satin-type fabric together, 12mm (½in) from the edge on the two long sides and one of the short sides. Turn to the right side, press gently and slip stitch the opening along the edge. Wrap the cover around the closed album and turn under the same amount to the inside of the album at the front and back to make the flap. Slip stitch at the top and bottom to make a removable jacket.

Gently steam press the embroidered fabric on the wrong side. Trim to 30cm × 23cm (12in × 9in), then turn under 12mm (½in) on all sides, mitring the

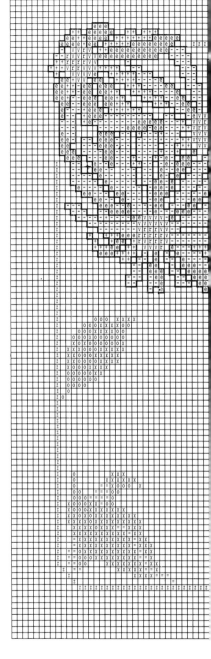

corners as explained on page 7. Position the embroidered panel centrally on the front of the cover and pin in place. Remove the cover from the album and baste and slip stitch the embroidered panel in place. Glue the lace daisies in place around the edge of the embroidered fabric. Replace the cover on the album.

On Your Diamond Wedding
May 26th
1995

Diamond Wedding Sampler

The soft cream and pink roses
on this sampler are a gentle
reminder of sixty happy years
spent together.

DIAMOND WEDDING SAMPLER

YOU WILL NEED

For the Diamond Wedding Sampler, with a design area measuring 18cm × 22.5cm (7in × 9in), or 123 stitches by 99 stitches, here in a frame measuring 23cm × 28cm (9¼in × 11in):

28cm × 33cm (11in × 13in) of cream, 14-count Aida fabric
Stranded embroidery cotton in the colours given in the panel
No24 tapestry needle
Strong thread, for lacing across the back
Cardboard, for mounting
Frame of your choice

•

THE EMBROIDERY

Prepare the fabric and stretch it in a frame as explained on page 5. Following the chart, start the embroidery at the centre of the design using two strands of cotton in the needle. Work each cross stitch over one block of fabric in each direction. Make sure that all the top crosses run in the same direction and that each row is worked into the same holes as the row before so that you do not leave a space between the rows. Add the appropriate date in dark beige and year in light beige, using the chart shown opposite for the alphabet and numbers.

MAKING UP

Gently steam press the finished embroidery on the wrong side and mount it as explained on page 7. Choose a mount and frame to compliment your embroidery colour and complete following the instructions on page 7.

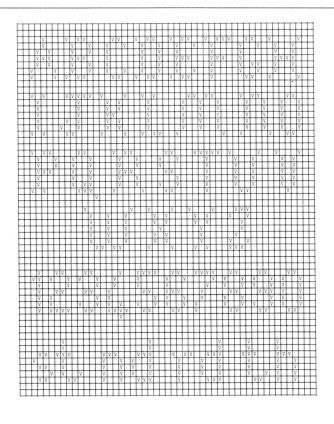

DIAMOND WEDDING SAMPLER ▶		DMC	ANCHOR	MADEIRA
s	Light green	3052	0861	509
╱	Medium green	3363	262	602
x	Dark green	3362	263	601
n	Light pink	776	025	0503
=	Dark pink	899	027	0505
e	Cream	746	0926	0101
<	Light beige	642	0392	1906
+	Dark beige	640	0393	1905
r	Blue	800	0128	0908
o	Yellow	3078	0292	0102

ACKNOWLEDGEMENTS

The author would like to thank the following people for their help with projects in this book:

Phoebe Spooner, Sharon Turner, Diana Jagger and especially Helen Burke.

Thanks are also due to DMC Creative World Ltd, for supplying fabrics, threads and card blanks; and Framecraft Miniatures Ltd, for supplying the serviette, traycloth, bowl and handbag mirror.

The bell pull fittings were supplied by: Crafts by Design, 28 Ederoyd Drive, Pudsey, West Yorkshire LS28 7RB. For details, send a stamped addressed envelope.

Enquiries about embroidery kits designed by Jane Alford under the Reflexions and Cross Purposes label may be sent to: Richard and Jane Alford, Reflexions/Cross Purposes, The Stables, Black Bull Yard, Welton, Lincoln LN2 3HZ.

SUPPLIERS

The following mail order company has supplied some of the basic items needed for making up the projects in this book

Framecraft Miniatures Limited
372-376 Summer Lane
Hockley
Birmingham B19 3QA
England
Telephone: 0121 359 4442

Addresses for Framecraft stockists worldwide

Ireland Needlecraft Pty Ltd
2-4 Keppel Drive
Hallam, Victoria 3803
Australia

Danish Art Needlework
PO Box 442, Lethbridge
Alberta T1J 3Z1
Canada

Sanyei Imports
PO Box 5, Hashima Shi
Gifu 501-62
Japan

The Embroidery Shop
286 Queen Street
Masterton
New Zealand

Anne Brinkley Designs Inc.
246 Walnut Street
Newton
Mass. 02160
USA

S A Threads and Cottons Ltd.
43 Somerset Road
Cape Town
South Africa

For information on your nearest stockist of embroidery cotton, contact the following:

DMC

UK
DMC Creative World Limited
62 Pullman Road
Wigston
Leicester LE8 2DY
Telephone: 0116 811040

USA
The DMC Corporation
Port Kearney Bld.
10 South Kearney
N.J. 07032-0650
Telephone: 201 589 0606

AUSTRALIA
DMC Needlecraft Pty
PO Box 317
Earlswood 2206
NSW 2204
Telephone: 02599 3088

COATS AND ANCHOR

UK
Coats Paton Crafts
McMullen Road
Darlington
Co. Durham DL1 1YQ
Telephone: 01325 381010

USA
Coats & Clark
PO Box 27067
Dept CO1
Greenville
SC 29616
Telephone: 803 234 0103

AUSTRALIA
Coats Patons Crafts
Thistle Street
Launceston
Tasmania 7250
Telephone: 00344 4222

MADEIRA

UK
Madeira Threads (UK) Limited
Thirsk Industrial Park
York Road, Thirsk
N. Yorkshire YO7 3BX
Telephone: 01845 524880

USA
Madeira Marketing Limited
600 East 9th Street
Michigan City
IN 46360
Telephone: 219 873 1000

AUSTRALIA
Penguin Threads Pty Limited
25-27 Izett Street
Prahran
Victoria 3181
Telephone: 03529 4400